Healthy Snack and Fast-Food *Choices*

consultant:
Lora A. Sporny, EdD, RD
Adjunct Associate Professor of Nutrition and Education
Teachers College, Columbia University

LifeMatters
an imprint of Capstone Press
Mankato, Minnesota

by
Mary
Turck

LifeMatters Books are published by Capstone Press
PO Box 669 • 151 Good Counsel Drive • Mankato, Minnesota 56002
http://www.capstone-press.com

Printed in the United States of America

Library of Congress Cataloging-in-Publication Data

Turck, Mary.
      Healthy snack and fast-food choices / by Mary Turck.
          p.   cm. — (Nutrition and fitness)
      Includes bibliographical references and index.
      ISBN 0-7368-0710-1
      1. Teenagers—Nutrition—Juvenile literature. 2. Snack foods—Juvenile literature. 3. Convenience
foods—Juvenile literature. 4. Food preferences—Juvenile literature. [1. Snack foods. 2. Nutrition.
3. Cookery.] I. Title. II. Series.
      RJ235 .T874 2001
      613.2′0835—dc21
                                        00-010200
                                        CIP

Summary: Discusses how to choose healthy snacks and fast foods in today's fast-paced world; inclu
recipes teens can make at home.

Staff Credits

Rebecca Aldridge, editor; Adam Lazar, designer and illustrator; Kim Danger, photo researcher

Photo Credits

Cover: The Stock Market/©Jose Pelaez
©Artville/Clair Alaska, 55
©DigitalVision, 35, 47
©Earthstar Stock, Inc., 15
International Stock/©Svoboda Stock, 6; ©James Davis, 17; ©Don Romero, 21; ©Jay Thomas, 58
Unicorn Stock Photos/©Martha McBride, 23; ©Jeff Greenberg, 25, 53; ©Eric R. Berndt, 57
Uniphoto/©Llewellyn, 8; ©Bob Daemmrich, 12; ©Gilmore J. Dufresne, 30; ©Jackson Smith, 38;
©Jonathan Taylor Photography, 48
Visuals Unlimited/©D. Cavagnaro, 29; ©Jeff Greenberg, 41; ©SIU School of Medicine, 44

A 0 9 8 7 6 5 4 3 2 1

Table of Contents

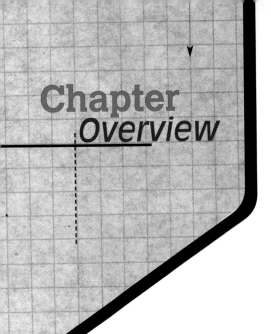

Chapter Overview

- Many people eat on the run because of their busy life.

- Fast food often is unhealthy. However, it can be nutritious if you make good choices.

- Snacks are an important part of your daily nutrition.

Chapter 1

Eating on the Run

Hurry and eat breakfast before the school bus arrives. Have a quick 20-minute lunch in the school cafeteria. Grab a snack after school to hold off hunger until dinnertime. Dinner itself is fast food again. This time it's from a drive-through window on the way to hockey practice or your part-time job. Does this sound like your day? If it does, you aren't alone.

Crowded schedules leave little time for enjoying a sit-down dinner. More than 66 million Americans eat at least one meal a day away from home. Many people eat these meals as they rush from place to place. The drive-through window often replaces the family dinner table.

You don't have to sacrifice good nutrition, even with today's fast-paced lifestyle. Nutrition is food that the body needs for growth, activity, and health. You can choose snacks and fast foods that provide good nutrition.

Fast Food

Fast food is big business around the world. Each fast-food restaurant has a meal it's known for. That meal may be a giant-sized burger and fries, or it may be tacos, pizza, or crispy fried chicken. All of these foods are high in calories, fat, and salt.

A fast-food burger often has a lot of calories and unhealthy fat and salt.

Julio, Age 17

Julio has just half an hour before beginning his afterschool job at a fast-food restaurant. He feels like he's starving. He orders a big burger and fries. He washes these down with a supersized diet cola. He feels much better. "Maybe at break time, I'll have a small chocolate shake," he thinks.

Julio's big burger had 560 calories, 1,070 milligrams of sodium from salt, and 31 grams of fat. His large order of fries had 450 calories, 290 milligrams of sodium, and 22 grams of fat. That's a lot of calories, sodium, and fat for one meal.

Calories

A calorie is the measure of the amount of energy a food gives the body. Most teens need about 2,200 to 3,000 calories every day. Extra calories not used for energy are stored in the body as fat. Therefore, eating too many high-calorie foods can cause people to become overweight. That means they have more body fat than is healthy. Julio's meal had 1,010 calories—about one-third to one-half of his calorie need for the entire day.

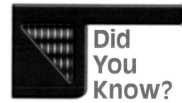
One gram of protein has four calories. One gram of carbohydrate has four calories. One gram of fat has nine calories.

Fat

The American Heart Association warns that eating a lot of high-fat food leads to heart disease. It says that people should get no more than 30 percent of their daily calories from fat. If Julio is eating 2,400 calories a day, that means no more than 720 of these calories should come from fat. One gram of fat has nine calories. That means he should be eating no more than 80 grams of fat each day. Julio's meal had 53 total grams of fat. That's two-thirds of his maximum daily fat in just one meal.

Sodium

Salt contains sodium. If the body gets too much sodium, that can lead to high blood pressure. It also can lead to loss of calcium into the urine, or the body's liquid waste. Dietary guidelines suggest eating no more than 2,400 milligrams of sodium daily. Julio's meal had 1,360 milligrams of sodium. That's more than half of the day's allowance.

A Variety of Choices

Today's fast-food chains offer many kinds of food. Besides their high-fat specials, their menus may list items such as broiled chicken and salads. That's good because greater variety usually means more nutritious choices.

Snacks

Teens eat lots of snacks. About 25 percent of a teen's daily calorie intake comes from snacks. That makes healthy snacks important because snacks can furnish a good part of the day's nutrition.

Fruit juice is a healthier choice than soda because it contains many needed vitamins.

Snacks can be loaded with nutrition. For example, milk and yogurt have lots of calcium and protein. The body needs these nutrients for strong muscles, bones, and teeth. Nutrients are the parts of food that the body needs for good health. Whole-grain breads, crackers, vegetables, and beans contain complex carbohydrates, also known as starches. Carbohydrates supply energy that the body needs. The body processes fiber-rich complex carbohydrates slowly. That means they offer long-lasting energy.

Some popular snacks do not offer good nutrition. Potato chips are high in salt and fat. Candy bars contain fat and sugar. Soda pop has lots of sugar. A 12-ounce (355-milliliter) can of soda contains about 40 grams of sugar. That's approximately 10 teaspoons of sugar!

Sugar, in all its forms, is a simple carbohydrate. The body processes simple carbohydrates quickly. They give a quick energy boost that's followed by a quick letdown. Sugars contain calories but no other nutrients. That's true for white sugar, brown sugar, corn syrup, fructose, honey, maple syrup, and most other kinds of sugar. Dark, or blackstrap, molasses, is an exception. This sugar contains a lot of calcium and iron. Calories from high-sugar foods are called empty calories.

Candy bars or soda may be occasional treats, but most of the time, snacks need to deliver more. When soda takes the place of milk or fruit juice, nutrition suffers. When empty calories replace nutrient-rich foods, health suffers.

Fast Fact

For a healthier alternative to soda, combine 8 ounces (240 milliliters) of fruit juice with 4 ounces (120 milliliters) of carbonated water.

Making Good Choices

Molly and Dyneisha, Age 14

Molly and her friend, Dyneisha, go to Molly's house after school. "I'm starving," Dyneisha says. "Do you want to share a chocolate bar? I've got one in my backpack. Do you have any pop?"

"We have plenty of snack stuff," Molly replies. "Would you like toasted multigrain bread with peanut butter? Or microwave popcorn? I can fix a fruit smoothie to drink. Or we could mix up some fruit juice and carbonated water."

Molly's snack ideas sound great! Multigrain bread and peanut butter offer protein, fiber, and many other nutrients. Fiber is important because it helps food move through the digestive system, keeping this system healthy. Popcorn is another good source of fiber. Fruit and fruit juices provide many vitamins. These nutritious snacks give a long, strong energy boost.

Molly and Dyneisha can choose empty calories or solid nutrition. The choice is up to them—and you.

Points to Consider

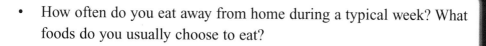

- How often do you eat away from home during a typical week? What foods do you usually choose to eat?

- Do you think your diet is healthy or unhealthy? Explain.

- What are your favorite grab-and-go snacks? Are they healthy? How could you make them healthier?

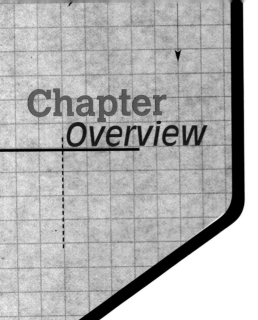

Chapter
Overview

- For good nutrition, everybody needs a variety of foods. Nutrition guides help people determine how much of each food group to eat daily.

- Most people need more vegetables, fruits, fiber, and water in their diet.

- Teens need extra calcium to support bone growth and strength.

- Teen girls need extra iron to replace iron lost in menstruation. Boys need extra iron to build lean muscle tissue.

- People who are lactose intolerant need to choose calcium-rich foods carefully.

Chapter 2

Nutrition Tips

Nutrition Guides

Nutrition guides help people choose foods wisely. The U.S. government created the Food Guide Pyramid as a guide to good nutrition. The Canadian government created a food rainbow called the Canadian Food Guide to Healthy Eating. Both give much the same nutrition guidance.

Processed foods carry labels that show nutritional content. These labels list the percent of recommended daily values that a particular food contains. Daily values allow people to compare the amount of nutrients in one serving of different foods.

Food guides and labels provide good information, but you still need to make choices. The food pyramid is based on adult nutrition needs. Daily values are based on a daily diet of 2,000 calories. Most active teens need to eat more than 2,000 calories. Teens need extra calories for growth and activity.

Choosing a Healthy Diet

The Food Guide Pyramid lists the number of servings people should eat daily to get all needed nutrients.

Bread, Cereal, Rice, and Pasta

The Food Guide Pyramid recommends 6 to 11 servings daily from the bread, cereal, rice, and pasta group. One slice of bread is a serving; so is a quarter of a bagel or half an English muffin. Half a cup (115 grams) of cooked rice or pasta equals one serving. When choosing foods from this group, it's best to consider whole-grain choices. Examples are whole-wheat bread, oatmeal or raisin-bran cereal, brown or wild rice, and multigrain crackers.

Vegetables and Fruits

Vegetables and fruits are on the same level of the Food Guide Pyramid. Everyone needs at least five servings a day from the fruit and vegetable groups. To help you, remember the phrase "Five a Day." That means having at least three vegetable servings and two fruit servings each day.

Everyone should eat three to five servings of vegetables each day. Half a cup (115 grams) of cooked vegetables is one serving. One cup (225 grams) of raw, leafy vegetables is a serving. Half a cup (115 grams) of chopped raw vegetables equals one serving.

Besides vegetables, the guide recommends two to four servings of fruit each day. Half a cup (115 grams) of cooked fruit or 6 ounces (177 milliliters) of fruit juice equals one serving. One medium-sized apple, banana, or orange is one serving.

Dairy

The Food Guide Pyramid recommends two to three servings of milk or other dairy products daily. That is about the right amount for adults. Teens need three to four servings of dairy every day. One cup (240 milliliters) of milk or 1 to 2 ounces (30 to 60 grams) of cheese makes one serving. One cup (225 grams) of yogurt equals a serving. When choosing dairy foods, it's best to consider low-fat and fat-free varieties.

Meat, Poultry, Fish, Beans, Eggs, and Nuts

The Food Guide Pyramid recommends two to three servings each day from the meat, poultry, fish, beans, eggs, and nuts group. One serving of meat is 2 to 3 ounces (60 to 85 grams) of cooked lean meat, poultry, or fish. This is a serving about the size of a deck of cards. One egg is a serving. Half a cup (115 grams) of cooked dry beans equals one serving. Two tablespoons (30 grams) of peanut butter equals a serving.

Fats, Oils, and Sweets

Fats, oils, and sweets are in the tiny section at the top of the pyramid. These aren't actually a food "group." Rather, these foods are needed in only very small amounts. People should eat very little of these foods.

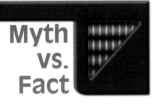

Myth: People need to take vitamin and mineral supplements for good health.

Fact: Most people who eat a well-balanced diet don't need supplements. Food is a better source of vitamins and minerals than supplements are. Food not only has the right balance of nutrients but also many other healthful substances.

Vegetables and Fruits—Not Just for Vegetarians

Jules and Ben, Ages 15 and 16

Jules is a vegetarian. She doesn't eat meat, fish, or poultry. Ben doesn't understand how Jules can give up cheeseburgers. "It's simple," she says. "I don't even want cheeseburgers anymore. I don't understand why you don't eat more vegetables. You know you need the vitamins." Ben admits that he doesn't eat enough vegetables. "I do eat fruit," he says, "but vegetables are boring."

Like Ben, most Americans do not eat enough vegetables. Only 1 person in 10 eats the recommended three to five servings a day. That leaves the majority of people short of essential vitamins, minerals, and other healthful plant substances called phytochemicals.

Vitamins and minerals don't provide calories for energy. Instead, the body uses small amounts of vitamins and minerals for specific functions. The body may use only small amounts, but these nutrients still are essential for good health. For example, vitamin A is needed for healthy skin and eyesight. Vitamin D helps absorb calcium and build bone.

Ben could quickly boost his nutrition by eating more vegetables. Eating just nine baby carrots would provide twice as much vitamin A as he needs in a day. Both salsa and spaghetti sauce provide vitamins A and C. Ben could drink a glass of tomato juice at lunch, eat a green salad at dinner, and snack on carrots. That would give him three vegetable servings.

Vegetables are an excellent source of vitamins, minerals, and fiber. They provide water, too.

Fruits furnish many needed nutrients, too. For example, raisins are high in iron. Oranges have lots of vitamin C. Mangoes and apricots are good sources of vitamin A.

Fiber and Water

People need fiber and water to regulate the activity of the digestive system. Nutrition guidelines recommend 20 to 35 grams of fiber daily. Most Americans eat less than half this amount, and many teens need more fiber in their diet. Fruits and vegetables provide fiber and water, as well as vitamins and minerals. Whole grains and beans provide fiber, vitamins, and minerals, too.

Vang, Age 15

Vang started gaining weight during his sophomore year. He talked with his doctor about diets. Dr. Sanchez said weight gain at Vang's age was normal. He said dieting wasn't a good idea. Instead, Dr. Sanchez suggested that Vang drink more water and eat more vegetables. Dr. Sanchez asked Vang to start drinking eight glasses of water each day.

Vang did. He drank at least a glass of water before each meal and snack. He felt less hungry and ate less. Next, Vang is going to focus on eating more vegetables.

Sometimes people feel hungry when all their body really needs is water. Often, drinking enough water helps people to eat less. Eating fruits and vegetables also helps fill you up.

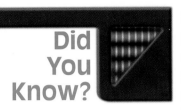

Did You Know?

Some people who are lactose intolerant drink soy milk made from soybeans. Other people may drink rice milk. Both soy milk and rice milk can be good sources of calcium if they are fortified with calcium. The label will tell you whether calcium has been added.

Special Teen Nutritional Needs

Teens need more calcium than adults. Bones grow rapidly during teen years, so teens need 1,300 milligrams of calcium every day to build strong bones. A cup (240 milliliters) of milk supplies 300 milligrams of calcium. A carton of yogurt supplies between 250 and 450 milligrams of calcium, depending on the variety.

Teens also use more iron than adults do. Teen boys need 12 milligrams of iron daily. They use extra iron to help build lean muscle mass. Teen girls need 15 milligrams of iron daily. They use extra iron to replace iron lost during menstruation. This is the monthly discharge of blood, fluids, and tissue from the uterus in nonpregnant females. The uterus is where an unborn baby develops. Good sources of iron are meats, poultry, clams, beans, tofu, broccoli, spinach, breakfast cereals, and dark molasses.

Lactose Intolerance

Milk contains lactose, which is a kind of sugar. Some people are lactose intolerant, meaning that they can't adequately digest lactose. Many Asian people are lactose intolerant. More African Americans than European Americans have lactose intolerance. People who are lactose intolerant do not digest milk well. Some of these people still can eat yogurt or cheese. Some can drink milk that has been specially processed to remove lactose. However, some cannot eat or drink any dairy products.

Because they're growing rapidly, teens need more calcium than most adults do.

Someone who is lactose intolerant must carefully choose dairy and nondairy foods to provide calcium. Some nondairy food choices that provide calcium are sardines, salmon, kale, collard greens, broccoli, and dark molasses. Cooked dried beans such as kidney beans, pinto beans, navy beans, and garbanzo beans also provide calcium.

Points to Consider

* How often do you think about good nutrition choices? What cues start you thinking about nutrition?

* The favorite vegetable of many teens is the potato. Potatoes are good for you, but French-fried potatoes have a lot of added sodium and fat. What other vegetables do you eat? What vegetables could you add to your daily diet?

* Do you think you get enough calcium? How could you add more calcium to your diet?

Chapter
Overview

- Fast-food meals can be healthy. Healthy fast-food choices include lean meats, whole-grain breads, low-fat or fat-free milk, fruits, and vegetables.

- Many fast foods are high in fat, sodium, and sugar.

- Even vending machines usually offer some healthy choices.

- You can make healthy fast-food choices.

Chapter 3

Fast-Food Choices

Winning Picks

Fast foods are not always junk foods. They can be nutritious. Many fast-food meals include a meat sandwich, French fries, and a soda. Meat provides needed protein. The bread in the sandwich supplies complex carbohydrates. Potatoes contain vitamins and carbohydrates. However, for balanced nutrition, more is needed. Two easy steps can add nutrition.

First, choosing low-fat or fat-free milk instead of soda adds calcium, vitamin D, and protein. This choice also cuts out the sugar in soda. (In the case of diet soda, it eliminates artificial sweeteners.)

Second, adding fruits or vegetables would boost nutrition by adding essential vitamins, minerals, and fiber. You can take along your own fruits and vegetables. Many kinds of fruit travel well. Hard fruits, such as apples, keep for a long time. Even soft fruits survive a day or two in a locker or backpack. Veggies can travel, too. Tomato juice comes in easy-to-carry cans. A handful of baby carrots can go in a plastic bag. Cherry tomatoes can be put in a small plastic container.

Fast Fact

Chicken skin contains most of the fat in chicken. Skinless chicken, especially white meat, usually is a low-fat choice.

Foods to Avoid

Fast foods often are high in sugar, sodium, and fat. Each of these substances can cause health problems. Making good choices means choosing less sugar, sodium, and fat.

Sodas contain high amounts of sugar. So do desserts. The average American eats 20 teaspoons (100 grams) of added sugar every day. Health experts say the limit on sugar should be no more than 10 teaspoons (48 grams) of added sugar a day.

Most cooked foods already contain salt. Adding more salt at the table further increases the sodium you get. French fries and processed meats such as ham or cold cuts have a lot of sodium.

When Fast Food Is Fat Food

Too much fat can clog arteries and add weight. It increases a person's chance for obesity, or weighing more than is healthy, and heart disease. Fried foods and most desserts are loaded with fat. Special sauces often are high in fat. Meats also contain fat. In general, beef has more fat than chicken. Dark meat chicken has more fat than light meat chicken does. However, there are exceptions to these general rules.

Pizza can contain a surprising amount of fat and salt.

The same piece of meat can have low or high fat, depending on how it's prepared. A broiled, skinless chicken breast may have only 2 grams of fat. The same chicken breast, breaded and fried, may have more than 30 grams of fat. Frying adds fat and breading soaks up even more fat during frying.

Pizza usually is high in fat and sodium. A single slice of a medium sausage pizza may have 17 grams of fat and 781 milligrams of sodium. A pizza made to serve one person often contains a lot of fat and sodium. It may contain twice as much as a pizza made to serve several people.

French fries and hot dogs usually have high fat and sodium content. Even a small order of fries has 12 grams of fat and 110 milligrams of sodium. A large order may double these amounts. A single hot dog may have 16 grams of fat and 700 milligrams of sodium.

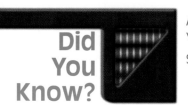

Did You Know?

American restaurants usually serve large portions. You almost always can divide a meal in half and share it or take half home for another meal.

Adding It Up

Malik, Age 17

Malik works at a nursing home three nights a week. On his way from school to work, he grabs a quick dinner. He usually stops at the same fast-food restaurant.

Malik often orders the special meal. This meal has a giant burger, a 16-ounce soft drink, and a large order of fries. For just 49 cents more, he can "supersize" the meal. That gives him a 32-ounce soft drink and a supersize order of fries.

Sometimes Malik supersizes his meal. Sometimes he orders just the giant burger and fries and a large milk. He doesn't do this often. The burger and fries and milk cost more than the special meal.

Like Malik, many people go for the bigger burger. That's the one we see advertised all the time. It's the one with special sauces, the one we need two hands to hold. It's the one we often learn to want.

The restaurant chain's special burger has lots of extras that add calories and fat. If Malik ordered two regular burgers, he would consume fewer calories. Two regular hamburgers would also deliver more protein with less fat than the giant burger.

Healthy Snack and Fast-Food Choices

Salad bars can provide plenty of healthy options. However, watch out for the fatty foods such as salad dressings and cheese.

Supersizing is a popular sales technique. For about 50 cents more, you can get a giant drink and fries instead of the regular size. That sounds like a good deal because you get more food for your money. However, more food doesn't mean better nutrition. A supersized soda delivers even more empty sugar calories than a regular-sized soda does. Supersized fries just give more fat and sodium than a smaller size does.

Salad Savvy

Vicky, Age 15

Vicky loves salad bars. She likes the feeling of healthy eating. She likes being able to go back for seconds or thirds. Vicky has a three-trip salad bar routine. First, she fills a plate with iceberg lettuce. Vicky tops the lettuce with tomatoes, croutons, cheese, and Thousand Island dressing. On her next trip, she loads up on pasta salads. She especially likes those with seafood. For her final plate, Vicky chooses fruit for her dessert.

Some fast-food restaurants have salad bars that offer many choices. A salad may sound super. For example, vitamins fill green and orange vegetables, and cottage cheese has calcium and protein. However, not all salad bar choices are great.

The biggest salad bar ambush is its high fat content. Vicky's pasta salads contain lots of fat and calories. Potato salads do, too. Salad dressings can turn green salads into fat traps. Two ounces (60 grams) of Thousand Island dressing have 11 grams of fat. Two ounces of low-fat French dressing have only four grams of fat. Low-fat dressings are a better choice than creamy dressings. Cottage cheese or vinegar and oil also make good salad toppings. Croutons, cheese, and black olives contain lots of fat. Lower-fat topping choices include tomatoes, carrots, onions, and other raw vegetables.

"Go for the green!" is good salad bar advice. The deeper green a vegetable is the more vitamins it contains. Romaine lettuce and spinach pack more nutrition than iceberg lettuce. If Vicky switches to a deeper green lettuce, she will boost the amount of vitamins she gets.

Vicky's fruit plate is a great dessert choice. With green salad and fruit, she is well on her way to a healthy "Five a Day!"

Vending Machines

Sometimes a snack, lunch, or even dinner comes from a vending machine. Most vending machine choices are high in salt or sugar. High-salt choices include peanuts and crackers. Candy, cookies, and bars have high sugar content.

Many vending machines offer better choices. One window may hold an apple or a hard-boiled egg. Another may offer yogurt. Sometimes machines have fruit juice or carbonated water, besides soda.

The snacks in a lot of vending machines are loaded with salt or sugar.

It's Up to You!

The best foods may be those that are homegrown and home-cooked. The best diet may be one that has many vegetables, fruits, and whole grains and that is low in fat. Unfortunately, most people do not eat the best food. Their diets are not perfectly balanced.

In real life, people cannot always make the best choice. Sometimes they choose between two less-than-perfect options. Fast food isn't the best food. But some fast foods are better than others. When you eat fast food, you have choices. You can avoid foods with lots of sugar, fat, and sodium. You can choose reasonable portion sizes. You can pack your own fresh fruits and vegetables. Making the best of fast-food eating is up to you.

Points to Consider

- What are the most healthy choices in your favorite fast-food restaurant? the least healthy?

- What fast-food ads are your favorites? What are the good and bad points of the foods they advertise?

- What are the three easiest things you could do to improve your fast-food meals?

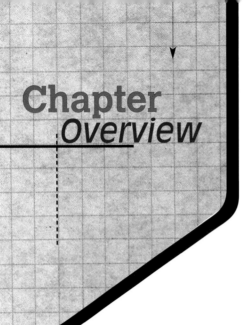

Chapter Overview

- Most teens need more calcium, vegetables, and fiber in their diet.

- Milk is the best source of calcium but not the only source.

- The darker the color of a vegetable, the more vitamins it contains.

- A variety of snacks provide fiber.

Chapter 4

Super Snacks

Calcium, Vegetables, and Fiber

Most teens need more calcium, vegetables, and fiber than they actually eat. (So do most adults!) The super snacks in this chapter feature these nutritional needs.

Cool Calcium

Milk can provide all the calcium people need. Sometimes plain milk may seem boring. Then it's time to try some cool calcium-rich snacks.

Pudding

Long ago, making pudding took time. You carefully stirred and cooked eggs, milk, and sugar. Today, pudding is a snap. Instant pudding mixes come with either sugar or artificial sweetener. You just add milk and stir for a few minutes. For variety, you can top with crushed graham crackers, nuts, toasted wheat germ, or dry cereal.

Frozen fruit makes smoothies easy. Just combine low-fat or fat-free milk and a cup (225 grams) of frozen berries and blend. Add a little chocolate syrup, dark molasses, or honey if the berries aren't sweet enough.

Yogurt Pops

Ingredients

2 cups (450 grams) plain, nonfat yogurt

2 tablespoons (30 grams) honey

½ teaspoon (2.5 milliliters) vanilla or almond extract

2 cups (450 grams) fresh or frozen fruit (strawberries, cherries, blueberries, or raspberries)

Directions

Place yogurt, honey, and vanilla or almond extract in a blender. Blend until thoroughly mixed. Add fruit. Run the blender in short bursts until fruit is in small pieces. Pour mixture into small paper cups. Insert a wooden stick or plastic spoon in the middle of each cup. Freeze until solid. Yogurt pops are cool, refreshing, and nutritious!

Smoothies

Ingredients

1 banana

1 tablespoon (15 grams) chocolate syrup

1 cup (240 milliliters) low-fat or fat-free milk

6 to 8 ice cubes

Directions

Put all ingredients in a blender. Blend until smooth and there you go! You have one milk and one fruit serving in a cool, delicious smoothie.

The darker green the lettuce, the more nutrients it contains.

Vibrant Veggies

Deep green, yellow, orange, and red vegetables pack vital vitamins. They make great snacks and are low in calories and fat.

Think Red!

Salsa packs a powerful punch, delivering vitamins A and C. A handful of low-fat corn chips and salsa makes eating veggies fun. One-half cup (120 milliliters) of salsa equals one vegetable serving.

Spaghetti sauce is a vegetable, too. Heat half a cup (120 milliliters) in the microwave and dip breadsticks in it for a quick pick-me-up.

Think Green!

One fast-food chain has salads you shake in a cup. You pour in the dressing, pop on the top, and shake the salad to mix. You can make your own less expensive kind at home.

Put salad ingredients in a large plastic container. Go for spinach or deep green lettuce such as romaine for maximum nutrition. Add shredded carrots, cherry tomatoes, and chopped cucumbers or other crunchy bits. Measure the dressing so you don't add too many fat calories. Shake and enjoy!

Making Vegetables Easy

Snacking is easier if veggies and dip are ready when you are. Wash and cut up vegetables. Then place them in plastic bags or containers in the refrigerator crisper drawer. Celery, carrots, and broccoli are familiar snacks, but green, red, and yellow bell peppers taste great, too.

Homemade muffins can be healthy snacks that provide needed fiber.

Fabulous Fiber

Fiber-rich foods can make great flavorful snacks. Think whole-grain crackers, nuts, and granola. Think popcorn with parmesan, cajun seasoning, or other toppings. Think raisins, figs, prunes, and dried apricots.

Muffins can be good snacks. Mega-muffins in restaurants may be loaded with fat and sugar. However, you can make maxi-muffins at home that are low in fat and high in fiber.

Maxi-Muffins

Ingredients

¾ cup (180 milliliters) low-fat or fat-free milk
¾ cup (170 grams) bran cereal
1 egg
¼ cup (60 milliliters) canola oil
¼ cup (60 grams) honey
¼ cup (60 grams) brown sugar
1 cup (225 grams) dry oatmeal
⅔ cup (150 grams) all-purpose white flour
1 tablespoon (15 grams) baking powder
¼ teaspoon (1 gram) salt
1 cup (225 grams) chopped walnuts, chopped dried fruit, or raisins

Healthy Snack and Fast-Food Choices

Directions

Turn on the oven to 400 degrees Fahrenheit (F) (200 degrees Celsius [C]). Lightly coat a muffin pan with cooking oil spray.

In a large bowl, combine the milk and bran cereal. Add the egg, oil, honey, and brown sugar. Beat with a hand mixer until smooth. Add the oatmeal, flour, baking powder, and salt. Beat until all the ingredients are moistened. Stir in the walnuts, raisins, or other dried fruit.

Spoon into muffin pans. Each muffin cup should be one-half to two-thirds full. Bake for 15 minutes at 400 degrees F (200 degrees C).

Test to see if the muffins are done. You can do this two ways. First, touch the top of a muffin lightly. If the imprint of your finger remains, they aren't done yet. If the muffin springs back, then they're done. Second, insert a clean toothpick in the middle of a muffin. Pull it out. Is it still clean or does it have a doughy glob on it? If the toothpick is clean, the muffins are done.

If the muffins aren't done, keep them in the oven. Test every 3 minutes until they're done. Let the muffins sit in the pan for 10 minutes after removing them from the oven. Then, enjoy!

Points to Consider

- At what times in the day do you want a snack? How could you prepare for these times?

- What are some other calcium-rich snacks you could make?

- What vegetables did you eat yesterday? What vegetables will you eat today? How nutritious do you think these vegetables are? Explain.

- How could you boost the amount of fiber in your daily diet?

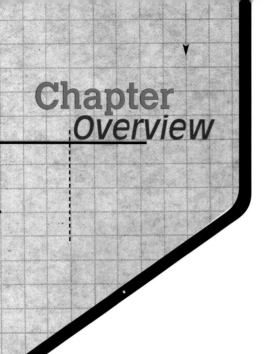

Chapter
Overview

- You can make incredibly tasty and nutritious snacks.

- Vegetables, tortillas, and fruits boost nutrition value.

- Preparing your own snacks saves money.

- Many healthy snacks travel well.

Chapter 5

Making Your Own Snacks

Making your own nutritious snacks at home is easy. You can make snacks that save you money and that are easy to carry with you. Any way you look at it, making your own snacks is a winning idea.

Eugenio, Age 16

Eugenio stocks shelves at a supermarket after school. He usually packs his own afterschool snack. He needs a high-energy snack to carry him through until supper.

Eugenio loves peanut butter. It gives him an energy and protein boost after school. Sometimes he fills celery sticks with peanut butter. He likes the combination of crisp and creamy textures. Sometimes he spreads a tortilla with peanut butter. Then he wraps it around a banana. That gives him fruit, grains, and nuts in an easy package.

Eugenio could buy a snack from the vending machine in the break room. However, packing his own snack saves him more than a dollar a day. His own snacks also are more nutritious than those in the vending machine.

Dip It!

Dips can be healthy snacks. They turn crackers, fruits, and vegetables into fun foods. Making dips that are good for you is easy. The key is beginning with nutritious ingredients. You can adjust the amount of each ingredient to get a taste you love.

Creamy Dips

Ingredients

1 cup (240 milliliters) reduced-fat mayonnaise
1 cup (225 grams) plain, nonfat yogurt
Seasonings to taste

Directions

Mix the mayonnaise and yogurt together. Add the seasonings you like best, but go easy on salt. Adding herbs boosts flavor without adding sodium. Here are four ideas for seasonings:

- Mince an onion and stir into the dip. (To mince means to cut or chop into very small pieces.) Add red pepper, garlic, or chili powder.

- Thaw a frozen package of chopped spinach. Squeeze the water out. Then add the spinach to the dip. Chop some water chestnuts and stir them in. Season with minced onion, garlic powder, basil, and black pepper.

- Peel a cucumber and slice it lengthwise. Scoop out the seeds and chop the cucumber. Add it to the yogurt-mayo combination. Season with dill and black pepper.

- Mince red and yellow bell peppers. Stir into the yogurt-mayo combination. Season with curry powder.

Refrigerate the dip for at least an hour. This gives the flavors time to blend.

Healthy Snack and Fast-Food Choices

Choose mild or hot peppers to turn the heat of your salsa down or up.

Salsa

Salsas can be tomato-based or fruit-based. They can be paired with bean dips rich in complex carbohydrates, protein, and fiber.

Homemade Salsa

Ingredients

3 tomatoes, peeled and chopped

1 onion, minced

2 cloves of garlic, minced

1 green bell pepper, seeded and diced

1 cayenne pepper, seeded and minced (carefully!) (Whenever you use hot peppers, wear rubber gloves while handling them. Their oils and juices can cause burns.)

1 teaspoon (5 milliliters) fresh-squeezed lime juice

Salt

Fresh, chopped cilantro

Directions

Stir together the tomatoes, onion, garlic, and peppers. Add lime juice and a little salt. Taste. Add more salt or lime juice to your own taste. Stir in cilantro. Refrigerate at least two hours so flavors blend.

For salsa variations, add chopped fruits. Try mangoes, peaches, and nectarines. Or, stir in well-drained canned corn, black beans, or pinto beans.

At a Glance

If you are using hot peppers, wear rubber gloves while handling them. Their oils and juices can cause burns. Never rub your eyes after slicing or touching a hot pepper.

Carbo Snacks

Foods containing complex carbohydrates make good snacks that provide long-lasting energy. Pasta, breads, rice, and cereals are complex carbohydrates that provide many snack possibilities. Choose cereal with milk for a bedtime snack as well as for breakfast. Top a chewy bagel with low-fat cheese or an all-fruit spread. Stuff pita bread with tomatoes, romaine lettuce, and shredded carrots. Or, try a tortilla. It can be used in many ways!

Ten Things to Do With a Tortilla

Tortillas come in many varieties. Corn tortillas and flour tortillas are traditional. Today, grocery stores also carry colorful red and green tortillas. These may have a little tomato or spinach added for color. Tortillas can be eaten in many different ways. Let these suggestions spark your imagination.

1. Use a pizza cutter to cut a tortilla into triangle-shaped pieces. Spray a cookie sheet with nonstick cooking spray. Then arrange the tortilla pieces on the cookie sheet and spray them, too. Sprinkle with a little chili powder, grated Parmesan cheese, seasoned salt, or some herbs. Bake in the oven at 350 degrees F (175 degrees C) until crisp. Dip your chips in salsa!

Healthy Snack and Fast-Food Choices

2. Spread mashed beans on a tortilla. Sprinkle with shredded, low-fat mozzarella cheese. Bake or microwave until the cheese melts.

3. Spread a thin layer of reduced-fat cream cheese over the tortilla. Top with whole or sliced berries. Fold in half and enjoy.

4. Spread the tortilla with a thin layer of reduced-fat cream cheese. Roll up a dill pickle in the tortilla.

5. Spread peanut butter on a tortilla. Sprinkle with raisins and cinnamon and roll up. Cut the rolled-up tortilla into half-inch (1.3-centimeter) pieces. Enjoy the peanut butter spirals!

6. Top a tortilla with peanut butter. Roll it around a peeled banana.

7. Try a tostada. Toast a tortilla until it's crisp. Top with lettuce, tomatoes, shredded low-fat cheese, and beans.

8. Invent a new taco. Fill your tortilla with leftovers from the fridge. Heat and eat.

9. A classic burrito starts with a large tortilla. Place a half-cup (115 grams) of mashed beans in the middle. Add low-fat cheese or salsa as desired. Roll up, folding ends shut.

10. You can eat a breakfast burrito any time of day. Scramble an egg and add low-fat cheese and beans. Roll it all up in a tortilla. This snack provides grain, dairy, and meat group servings. Half a cup (115 grams) of salsa would add a vegetable serving, too!

Cut up and bag vegetables or prepare other snacks ahead of time. Then, you can just reach in the refrigerator for a quick and portable snack.

On the Go

Jessica, Age 13

Jessica crammed her math book into her backpack. It was 7:15 A.M. She had to catch the bus at 7:25. After school, she had to go to the library. What could she take along for an afternoon snack?

She opened the refrigerator. The large plastic snack box held apples, small bags of carrots, and cheese sticks. She grabbed two cheese sticks and an apple and ran out the door.

Like many people, Jessica needed to grab a snack quickly. She didn't have time to stop and prepare one. Luckily, her family kept a big box of snacks ready to go.

Healthy Snack and Fast-Food Choices

Before peeling tomatoes, dunk each one in boiling water for about 10 seconds. Be careful! Use a metal cooking basket or slotted spoon to do this. Next, plunge the tomato into cold water. Now use your fingers to slide the skin off the tomato.

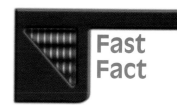

Fast Fact

Keeping healthy snacks on hand is easy. One container can hold refrigerated snacks. Another can keep snacks organized in the pantry or in a cupboard. When you need a snack, you can grab one and go!

Many healthy snacks travel well. Crackers, pretzels, and popcorn go anywhere. To save money, buy a large box of pretzels or crackers. Then repack them in snack-size plastic bags.

Buying in quantity saves money. A bag of a dozen apples may cost $2.29. That's less than 20 cents per apple. Apples from a vending machine usually cost at least 50 cents each. Buying a single apple in a cafeteria may cost even more. One large package of crackers costs less in the long run than a package of only a dozen crackers. Buying in quantity helps the environment, too. Single-serving sizes use more packaging material than large sizes do.

If you refrigerate an unpeeled onion for an hour, you won't "cry" when peeling and chopping it.

Dried fruits and nuts make good take-along snacks. You can eat them plain or as part of granola, which is nutritious and easy to make.

Granola

Ingredients

4 cups (900 grams) dry oatmeal
½ cup (115 grams) chopped nuts
½ cup (115 grams) unsalted sunflower seeds (shelled)
½ cup (115 grams) honey
¼ cup (60 milliliters) canola oil
1 teaspoon (5 milliliters) vanilla or almond extract
½ teaspoon (2 grams) cinnamon
½ teaspoon (2 grams) salt
1 cup (225 grams) raisins or dried cranberries
1 cup (225 grams) dried apricots, chopped

Directions

Preheat oven to 350 degrees F (175 degrees C).

In a large bowl, mix oatmeal, nuts, and sunflower seeds. In a small bowl, combine honey, oil, vanilla or almond extract, cinnamon, and salt. Mix well. Drizzle over oatmeal mixture. Stir to mix well. Then, spread on a baking sheet.

Bake until golden brown, gently turning the mixture with a spatula every 10 minutes. This will take approximately 30 to 40 minutes. Remove from oven. Pour mixture into a bowl, and stir in fruit. Cool completely. Store in a tightly covered container.

Whether making granola or cooking something else that needs oil, use canola oil. Of all oils, it's lowest in artery-clogging saturated fat.

The following are some other ideas for take-along snacks. Use your imagination to come up with more portable snack ideas.

- A can of fruit juice

- Graham crackers spread with peanut butter

- A small carton of yogurt

- Thinly sliced cheese and rye crackers

Points to Consider

- How can making your own snacks save money?

- What snacks do you already make at home? Are they healthy? Why or why not?

- What snacks would you like to try making at home? Do you think this would be easy or difficult? Explain.

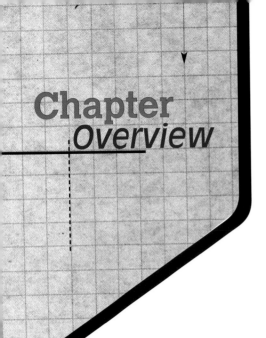

Chapter Overview

- Advertising usually does not provide important nutrition information.

- Food labels give nutrition information.

- Not all "light" snacks are created equal.

- Fresher foods contain fewer chemicals.

Chapter 6

Help for Healthy Choices

Advertising vs. Information

You need good information to make good nutrition choices. Most advertising doesn't give good information. Ads work by hooking your emotions, not your intelligence.

Advertising often encourages overeating, which can lead to weight gain. Foods in ads are bigger and better. Pizzas have more cheese. Burgers are so big you need both hands to hold them. Candy bars are jumbo size.

Ads often sell foods that have little nutritional value, such as candy, potato chips, and soda pop. Foods in ads often have high sugar, fat, and sodium content.

People often tune out advertising. They know that ads are there to sell products. During commercials, they may talk or check out the refrigerator, but they still hear the ads. The messages still reach their mind.

Sometimes advertising is hidden. You may be watching a favorite TV program. The characters talk in the living room where two cans of soda pop sit on the table. One of the characters orders a pizza. The brand names for the soda and pizza are visible. This is called product placement, and it can influence people just like commercials do.

A food that says it's lower in fat may still contain a lot of fat and calories.

In contrast to advertisements, food labels give solid information. The label tells whether a drink is 100 percent juice and how much sugar it contains. The label tells how much sodium and fat are in a bag of potato chips.

You make your own nutrition choices. Food labels give you information on which to base those choices that shape both your body and your health.

Read the Label

Moua, Age 14, and Mai, Age 17

Moua and Mai do the family grocery shopping. They choose snacks for the whole family. Last week, Moua suggested that they try the new, fat-free potato chips. "Less fat is better," she reminded her older sister.

"That's true," Mai replied, "but I don't trust these. Look at the ingredients." Together, the sisters read the label.

"Look," said Mai. "There's a fat substitute I've read about. It has some nasty side effects. We won't buy these."

"Good point," said Moua. "Let's find another way to cut down on fat."

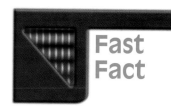

Chips usually have high salt and fat content. Still, not all chips have the same amount of fat. Moua is right to look for chips with less fat. Mai is right, too. She knows that these fat-free chips have other problems. Reading labels helps people make good choices.

Moua and Mai see that one brand of crackers contains 1.5 grams of fat in a serving of five crackers. A second brand has 4 grams of fat in the same size serving. One bag of potato chips has 8 grams of fat in a serving of 12 to 15 chips. A bag of tortilla chips shows 6 grams of fat per serving. A bag of baked tortilla chips has only 4 grams.

Mai and Moua decide against the potato chips. Everyone in the family likes potato chips, and they don't stop eating after just 12 chips. So for their family, eating potato chips means eating a lot of fat.

Mai and Moua also leave the crackers on the shelf. No one in the family really likes crackers. They don't want to buy nutritious food that no one likes. They decide to buy baked tortilla chips instead.

"Light" Snacks

Food labels and ads carry many health claims to sell snacks. They may contain the words *light, lite, low-fat, reduced fat,* or *low-calorie*. What do such claims mean?

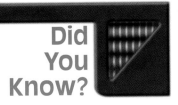
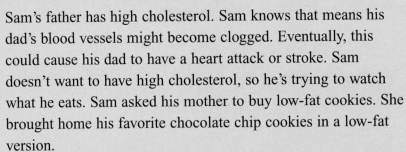

Sam and Jamar, Age 15

Sam's father has high cholesterol. Sam knows that means his dad's blood vessels might become clogged. Eventually, this could cause his dad to have a heart attack or stroke. Sam doesn't want to have high cholesterol, so he's trying to watch what he eats. Sam asked his mother to buy low-fat cookies. She brought home his favorite chocolate chip cookies in a low-fat version.

Sam went to Jamar's house to study for a world geography test. He took along the box of low-fat cookies. Jamar said he didn't want any. "I'm trying to cut down on calories," Jamar told his friend. "Your cookies are low-fat, but they're high in sugar. I don't need the extra calories from sugar!" Sam was surprised to find that his cookies had so much sugar and so many calories.

Consumers need to know what health claims mean. United States law sets some limits on the claims "low-fat" and "light." Low-fat means less than 3 grams of fat per serving. Like Sam's cookies, these foods may still be high in calories. They just have lower fat content.

Sugar is hidden in many foods, including some spaghetti sauces!

Light or lite foods must have one-third fewer calories than their regular version. That doesn't mean they are low in fat or in calories. Ice cream is a good example. A half-cup (115-gram) serving of ice cream may have 160 calories and 9 grams of fat. A light version could still have 106 calories and 6 grams of fat.

Sugar, Sugar, Everywhere

Sugar occurs naturally in many foods. The natural sugar in milk and fruit comes along with vitamins and minerals. The added sugar in ice cream or fruit punch doesn't add any nutrition. Extra sugar just adds empty calories. The average American eats more than 150 pounds (68 kilograms) of sugar each year. Much of that sugar is hidden in food.

Most people know soda is high in sugar. Fruit drinks and fruit juices have high sugar, too. Fruit drinks usually have added sugar. Some juices are naturally high in sugar. Often sugar is added to fruit juice blends. It adds sweetness without adding much nutrition.

Sugar is added to many other foods as well. Many sweetened breakfast cereals contain 3 or 4 teaspoons (15 or 20 grams) of sugar per serving. Baked goods often have lots of added sugar.

Sometimes sugar is hidden where it's least expected. Some peanut butter brands have added sugar. Many spaghetti sauces do as well.

It's important to wash fruits and vegetables thoroughly before you eat them.

Chemical Carnival

Many packaged foods contain added chemicals. These chemicals have many confusing names. Xanthum gum, tetrasodium, pyrophosphate, monoglycerides, diglycerides, acesulfame potassium, GHA, and TBHQ are just a few. What on earth are these things? Some chemicals help foods last longer on the shelf. Some improve the way foods look or taste.

Scientists test the chemicals used in food. They make sure that the chemicals are safe to eat. Many people still prefer to avoid them. Fresh foods contain fewer added chemicals than processed foods do. If you want to avoid chemicals, eat more fresh foods.

Healthy Snack and Fast-Food Choices

Myth: Fresh fruits and vegetables are dangerous. They have been sprayed with lots of pesticides, or chemicals that kill insects.

Fact: Avoiding fresh fruits and vegetables is a bigger danger to your health. Simply wash fresh fruits and vegetables well when you bring them home.

Myth
vs.
Fact

Points to Consider

- Let's say you're making a grocery list. What foods that you'd use to make snacks would you put on it?

- Check the labels on three of your favorite foods. What is the sugar content of each one? Is this a surprise? Why or why not?

- How do you feel about chemicals used in foods? Explain.

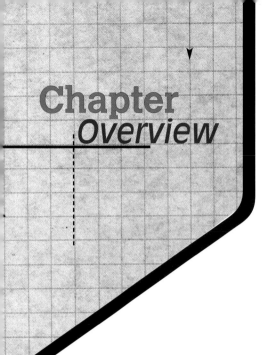

Chapter Overview

- Great snacking starts at home.

- Healthy snacking is a family affair.

- You can share nutritious snacks with friends.

- Party food can be healthy food. You can learn ways to stay in control of eating at a party.

- Your healthy snack choices are part of a healthy lifestyle.

Chapter 7

The Right Mix for You

Ready, Set, Snack!

You come home from school, tired and hungry. You look in the kitchen. What do you find?

Brianna, Age 16

Brianna often had milk and cookies after school, but she wanted to add more fruits and vegetables to her diet. Her mother suggested replacing milk and cookies with a fruit or vegetable snack.

Brianna went to the grocery store. She bought precut carrots, cauliflower, and broccoli. She made a yogurt-based dip. Now reaching for a veggie snack was easy! After a week, veggies and dip seemed boring. Brianna began looking for new ideas.

The grocery store offers many snack choices. Brianna could choose low-fat string cheese and high-fiber crackers. She could drink tomato juice or a vitamin-packed juice combination. Crispy, sweet parsnips, brightly colored bell peppers, high-fiber celery, and prepared salads are other snacks in the vegetable aisle.

Brianna's mom washes fruits as soon as she brings them home. A fruit bowl on the kitchen table keeps apples, pears, and bananas ready to eat.

A variety of choices in Brianna's kitchen make healthy snacking easier. Cookies, granola bars, and microwave popcorn sit on a cupboard shelf. So do three kinds of low-fat crackers. Cookies are not really a healthy snack, but they are still there when Brianna wants to splurge, or indulge.

Family Food Choices

Families can make good nutrition easy or hard. Sometimes a family's pantry holds fruit and whole-grain crackers. The refrigerator may have milk, cheese, and two kinds of fruit juice. It also may have a fruit salad made from diced pineapple, mangoes, strawberries, and cantaloupe. This makes eating healthy snacks easy. Sometimes the pantry holds potato chips and cupcakes. In the refrigerator, a bottle of soda may sit beside the milk carton. This can make healthy choices hard.

Healthy snacking is easier to do if your family keeps nutritious foods around.

Damon, Age 14

Every day after school, Damon takes care of his younger sisters. He fixes them a snack and supervises homework. The girls get home from school at 3 P.M. Their mom gets home from work at 6 P.M.

Damon's sisters like sweet snacks. They prefer cookies and candy. Damon likes sweets, too. But he cares about good nutrition. He offers his sisters fresh fruit instead of cookies. He gives them granola bars instead of candy. He insists that his sisters drink milk or fruit juice as part of their snack.

Friday is a day to relax. Then, they celebrate with milk and cookies.

Healthy eating is a family affair. Damon's cupboards hold healthy snacks. His family also follows a routine. His sisters know the routine. Friday is the day for cookies. They don't ask for cookies on other days.

Once in a while, most people like to splurge. That's why Damon and his sisters enjoy their cookies on Friday. They eat nutritious food most of the time, so an occasional splurge won't hurt.

Some cookies are healthier than others. The sandwich cookies from the store have a filling that is simply sugar and fat. Homemade chocolate chip cookies taste better and can be better for you. The oatmeal and whole-wheat flour in the following recipe add healthy fiber. The applesauce adds moisture to the cookies, which allows for less oil to be used in the recipe.

Chocolate Chip Cookies

Ingredients

¾ cup (170 grams) whole-wheat flour, unsifted
¾ cup (170 grams) all-purpose white flour, unsifted
1 teaspoon (5 grams) baking soda
½ cup (120 milliliters) canola oil
½ cup (115 grams) unsweetened applesauce
1 cup (225 grams) brown sugar
1 teaspoon (5 milliliters) vanilla
2 eggs
2 cups (450 grams) dry oatmeal
1 package semisweet chocolate chips

Directions

In a small bowl, mix together whole-wheat flour, white flour, and baking soda. In a large bowl, combine the oil, applesauce, brown sugar, vanilla, and eggs. Beat together with a hand mixer until smooth. Add the flour mixture to the wet ingredients. Continue to beat until well blended. With a large spoon or rubber spatula, stir in oatmeal and chocolate chips. Drop by large spoonfuls onto ungreased cookie sheet. Bake at 350 degrees F (175 degrees C) for 8 to 10 minutes. Let cookies sit on cookie sheet for 2 minutes after you take them out of the oven. Then, place cookies on wire rack to cool. Enjoy!

By sharing healthy snacks with friends, you share good health.

Sharing Good Health

In elementary school, many kids trade items from their lunches. Now that you're older, you can still share food with friends. Sharing nutritious snacks means sharing good health.

Tessa, Age 13

Tessa's parents insist on healthy meals for the family. Tessa packs her own lunch and snack every day. Sometimes she wishes that she had potato chips or candy bars. But her family's pantry and refrigerator offer only healthy choices.

Tessa enjoys sharing snacks with her friends. Sometimes she brings an extra apple or bag of trail mix to share. String cheese and rye crackers also are favorites.

Tessa's parents buy food for good nutrition. Her friends share and enjoy the food because it tastes good.

One of Tessa's favorite snacks is trail mix. This is a versatile snack. It can take many different forms. For example, some people don't like nuts. Those people can just leave out the nuts. Other people love chocolate. They can increase the amount of chocolate chips. Do you love dried cherries? Add a handful. Following is a starter recipe for trail mix. You can adjust it to your own personal taste.

Some party food ideas include fresh fruit kabobs, air-popped popcorn, and low-fat, whole-grain crackers with low-fat cheese squares.

delicious

Trail Mix

Ingredients

Round-shaped oat cereal

Pretzels (minipretzels or skinny pretzel sticks)

Dry-roasted peanuts

Sunflower seeds (shelled)

Mini-chocolate chips

Mixed nuts

Raisins or currants

Dried apples or apricots, chopped

Banana chips

Directions

Measure out one cup (225 grams) of each ingredient. Mix together. Store in a tightly closed container in a dry place. Or divide in small, sealable plastic bags before storing. That will give you a grab-and-go snack.

Party Snacks

Party time can seem like pig-out time, but it doesn't have to be that way. Many party tables offer a variety of foods. One simple move guarantees great-tasting, healthy party food. Bring some yourself! Trail mix and popcorn make great party foods. So does a plate of sliced fruit with a special dip.

Parties can make healthy eating seem challenging. However, several tips can help you.

Party Plate

Stir 3 tablespoons (45 grams) of honey and ½ teaspoon (2.5 milliliters) of almond extract into a cup of plain, nonfat yogurt. Slice three apples and three pears.

Put the dip in a dish in the middle of a colorful plastic plate. Arrange the fruit slices around the edge of the plate. Serve and enjoy!

Staying in Control

A table loaded with snacks is hard to resist. A few strategies can help you stay in control of party eating.

- **Eat before you go.** Have a bowl of soup, a slice of whole-grain bread, or a big salad. Drink a glass of fat-free milk, too. It's easier to stay in control if you aren't starving!

- **Pass on sugary soda.** Drink sparkling water or fruit juice. If you fill up on sparkling water, you won't be so hungry for nachos or other party food.

- **Get involved with something besides food.** Find old friends or make a new friend. Look through the music choices. Play a game or dance. Some people eat because of boredom. Don't be one of them!

- **Stay away from the food table.** Just seeing food makes most people want to eat more.

Martin knows that eating right helps him to play his best.

In Training for Life

Martin, Age 16

Martin plays soccer. He takes it very seriously. He is a good athlete.

During soccer season, Martin is in training. He runs, practices, and eats right. He chooses his meals and snacks carefully. He wants good nutrition and high energy.

"If I don't eat well, I can tell the difference," he says. "I feel better and perform better when I eat right."

Martin depends on his body. He needs to be able to run and move with ease. He needs high energy levels. He wants to be a star. He eats right so that he can perform well. Athletes like Martin know they need good nutrition. Their body works better with good nutrition.

Healthy Snack and Fast-Food Choices

College athletes often eat at a special training table. They need good nutrition and lots of it. Their training table has more food—and sometimes better food—than the rest of the cafeteria.

We are all in training for life. We all need good nutrition for health, growth, and strength. Like athletes in training, we can make good nutrition choices.

Points to Consider

- What snack ideas would you suggest to Brianna?

- What healthy snacks do your friends enjoy?

- What are the best homemade party snacks that you have eaten?

- How does your family make healthy snacking easier or harder?

- If you were an athlete, would you eat differently than you do now? Why or why not?

Note

Internet Sites

The Healthy Refrigerator
www.healthyfridge.org
Contains information and recipes for heart-healthy eating and general nutrition for children and teens

KidsHealth.org
www.kidshealth.org/teen/nutrition/menu/healthy_snacks.html
Contains article about snacking for teens

Lambton Health Unit
www.lambtonhealth.on.ca/nutrition/snacksgrde.htm
www.lambtonhealth.on.ca/nutrition/eatingout.htm
Contains articles on being healthy when snacking and eating out

Vegetarian Recipes Around the World
www.vegsource.com/vegunion/recipes/snacks
Has recipes for many different vegetarian snacks

For More Information

Useful Addresses

American Dietetic Association (ADA)
216 West Jackson Boulevard
Chicago, IL 60606-6995
1-800-877-1600
www.eatright.org

Center for Science in the Public Interest
1875 Connecticut Avenue Northwest
Suite 300
Washington, DC 20009-5728
www.cspinet.org

Health Canada
Health Promotions and Programs Branch
Nutrition and Healthy Eating Program
Jeanne Nance Building, Tunney's Pasture
Ottawa, ON K1A 1B4
CANADA
www.hc-sc.gc.ca

For Further Reading

Bennett, Paul. *Eating Healthy.* Parsippany, NJ: Silver Press, 1998.

Gregson, Susan R. *Healthy Eating.* Mankato, MN: Capstone, 2000.

Schwager, Tina, and Michele Schuerger. *The Right Moves: A Girl's Guide to Getting Fit and Feeling Good.* Minneapolis: Free Spirit, 1998.

Warner, Penny. *Healthy Snacks for Kids.* San Leandro, CA: Bristol Publishing, 1996.

Glossary

calcium (KAL-see-uhm)—nutrient needed to build and maintain bone strength

calorie (KAL-uh-ree)—a measurement of the amount of energy that a food contains

carbohydrate (kar-boh-HYE-drate)—a nutrient that provides energy

cholesterol (kuh-LESS-tuh-rol)—a waxy substance made by animals, including humans; it's needed to make vitamin D and other body chemicals and tissues.

complex carbohydrate (KOM-pleks kar-boh-HYE-drate)—a carbohydrate that is digested slowly and provides long-lasting energy

fat (FAT)—an oily nutrient found in the body tissue of animals and some plants

fiber (FYE-bur)—a part of plant foods that is not digested which helps food move through the intestines

iron (EYE-urn)—a mineral the body needs for healthy, oxygen-rich blood

lactose (LAK-tohss)—a kind of sugar found in milk

mince (MINSS)—to cut or chop into very small pieces

nourishment (NUR-ish-muhnt)—food substances necessary to maintain life

nutrient (NOO-tree-uhnt)—a substance in foods that is needed to help the body grow, stay healthy, and repair itself

simple carbohydrate (SIM-puhl kar-boh-HYE-drate)—sugar that is digested and absorbed quickly for short-term energy

sodium (SOH-dee-uhm)—a part of salt; having too much sodium can cause high blood pressure.

vitamin (VYE-tuh-min)—a nutrient needed for growth and health

Index

advertising, 22–23, 43, 44, 45
American Heart Association, 7

beans, 8, 13, 15, 16, 17, 35, 37
beverages. *See* fruit juices; soda
bread, 8, 9, 12, 19, 29, 36
burgers, 5, 6, 14, 22, 43. *See also* meat

calcium, 7, 8, 14, 16–17, 19, 23, 27
calories, 5, 6, 7, 11, 14, 22–24, 29, 44, 46–47
    empty, 8, 9, 23, 47
Canadian Food Guide to Healthy Eating, 11
candy, 8, 9, 24, 43, 53, 55. *See also* dessert; sweets
carbohydrates, 7
    complex, 8, 19, 35, 36
    simple, 8
cereal, 12, 16, 27, 30–31, 36, 47, 56
chemicals, 48, 49
chips, 8, 29, 43, 44–45, 52, 55. *See also* fried foods
choices, 5, 7, 11, 12–15, 25, 58, 59
    family food, 52–54
    fast-food, 5, 19–25
    help for healthy, 43–49
    snack, 7–9
cholesterol, 46
cookies, 24, 46, 51, 52, 53–54. *See also* sweets
crackers, 8, 12, 24, 27, 30, 34, 39, 41, 45, 52, 55, 56

dairy, 8, 13, 16–17, 37. *See also* milk
dessert, 20, 23, 24, 47. *See also* candy; cookies; fruits; sweets
dips, 34, 51

eggs, 13, 24, 27, 30–31, 37, 54
energy, 6, 8, 9, 14, 33, 36, 58

fast food, 5–7, 22–23. *See also* fried foods; pizza
    choices, 5, 19–25
fat, 5–7, 13, 20–25, 29, 30, 34, 36, 37, 43, 44–47, 54
fiber, 8, 9, 15, 19, 27, 30, 35, 54
fish, 13, 14, 17
Food Guide Pyramid, 11, 12–13
foods to avoid, 20. *See also* fast food
fried foods, 5, 6, 19, 20–21, 23. *See also* chips; fast food
fruit juices, 8–9, 13, 24, 41, 47, 57
fruits, 12–15, 19, 23–25, 28, 30, 34, 35, 36, 37, 39, 47, 48, 49, 51–53. *See also* dessert

granola, 30, 40
granola bars, 52, 53

heart disease, 7, 20, 46
high blood pressure, 7

information, 43, 44
iron, 15, 16

labels, 11, 13, 16, 44, 45, 46
lactose intolerance, 16–17

meat, 13, 14, 16, 19–21, 37, 43. *See also* burgers
milk, 13, 16, 27, 28, 30, 36, 47, 52, 57. *See also* dairy
minerals, 14–15, 19, 47
molasses, 8, 16, 17, 28
muffins, 30–31
myths, 14, 49

Index

nutrients, 8, 9, 11, 13–15
nutrition, 5, 8, 23, 43, 58, 59
    teen, 16
    tips, 11–17
nuts, 13, 27, 30, 33, 40, 55, 56

oils, 13, 24

pasta, 12, 36
peanut butter, 9, 13, 33, 41, 47
phytochemicals, 14
pizza, 5, 21, 43. *See also* fast food
plastic bags, 19, 29, 38–39
popcorn, 9, 30, 39, 52, 56
poultry, 7, 13, 14, 16, 20–21
processed foods, 11
protein, 7, 8, 19, 22–23, 33, 35
pudding, 27

recipes
    chocolate chip cookies, 54
    creamy dips, 34
    granola, 40
    homemade salsa, 35
    maxi-muffins, 30–31
    party plate, 57
    smoothies, 28
    tortillas, things to do with, 36–37
    trail mix, 56
    yogurt pops, 28
rice, 12, 16, 36
routines, 5, 53

salads, 7, 14, 23–24, 29, 57. *See also*
        vegetables
salsa, 14, 29, 35, 36, 37
salt, 5, 6, 20, 21, 24. *See also* sodium
serving sizes, 5, 6, 12–13, 22–23, 25
sharing, 55

smoothies, 9, 28
snacks, 5, 7–9, 52, 53
    "light," 45–47
    making your own, 25, 33–41
    party, 56–57
    super, 27–31
soda, 6, 8, 9, 19, 20, 23, 43, 47, 52, 57
sodium, 6, 7, 20, 21, 23, 25, 43, 44.
        See also salt
starches. *See* carbohydrates, complex
sugar, 8, 16, 19, 20, 23–25, 30, 43, 44,
        46–47, 54, 57
supplements, 14
sweets, 13, 28, 53. *See also* candy;
        cookies; dessert

tacos, 5, 37
tortillas, 33, 36–37, 45
trail mix, 55–56
training, 58–59

vegetables, 8, 12, 13, 14–17, 19,
        23–25, 27, 29, 33–34, 35, 36,
        37, 38–39, 48, 49, 51–52. *See
        also* salads
vegetarians, 14
vending machines, 24, 25, 33, 39
vitamins, 9, 13, 14–15, 19, 23–24, 29,
        47

water, 15
weight gain, 6, 15, 20, 43
whole grains, 8, 12, 15, 25, 30, 52

yogurt, 13, 16, 24, 28, 34, 41, 57
yogurt pops, 28